# FOOTPRINTS

*"Where Life Begins
and Love Never Ends"*

## MALCOLM ALLEN

# FOOTPRINTS

To all the single parents...
NEVER GIVE UP!

# CONTENTS

# INTRODUCTION:
# AN HONEST LETTER TO SINGLE MOMS

To single moms everywhere:

We are the fathers of your children. Some of you haven't seen much of us lately, but we are here. We include fathers everywhere.

Some of you have seen the best among us, only to lose us. Many of us always embraced fatherhood, spending time with our children every day. We worked difficult jobs to support them. We worked with you, their mothers, to find good schools, make our neighborhoods safe, and give our kids a world where they could thrive. Then something happened—an illness, accident, or a criminal's bullet—and we were gone. We didn't want to leave you alone, but no one gave us a choice.

Then there are those among us, still living, who haven't always done the right thing. You needed men who would stay, but some of us walked away. Some of us have spent time in prison. Some of us have fathered your children, then hung around doing nothing. Too many of us have cashed your paychecks, left the kids with Grandma, and spent your money on drugs, alcohol, or other women. Then we came home, looking for more opportunities to grab something for free. A few of us may be beyond help; the rest of us should be helping you rather than hurting you. Some of us are finally ready to do that. We are ready to learn how to be the good fathers our children need us to be.

You have a right to expect that, and more, from those of us who are still here in this world. We haven't been there for you, or for our children. If we'd done the right thing, and stayed, you wouldn't be single moms. Each morning you wake up to another day when we're not there changing diapers, taking the kids to the doctor, or driving them to school. You do all that. After working all day to support them, you come home to the full-time job of motherhood. You get them to do their homework, and you talk to their teachers. You tell them bedtime stories, and they tell you their dreams.

When they are sick, you nurse them. If you need someone else to watch them, it's up to you to call your mom, or sister, or neighbor. If you can hire a babysitter, you are the one who pays. You are the one who tries to save money for their future. You take all the responsibility. In return, you get their love. Despite all the work, that sounds like a great payback, and it is, but love is so much greater when two parents can share it.

Love can't be measured in numbers, but the math can tell us a lot about responsibility—who's taking it, and who's not. According to the U.S. Department of the Census, 43.1% of all children live without their fathers. That's almost half the children we see each day. This repeats itself generation after generation. Seventy-one percent of pregnant teenage girls don't have a father at home. Fatherless homes produce other problems. Three-quarters of the adolescents in drug treatment facilities are fatherless. The same is true of 71% of the high school dropouts, 85% of the children with behavioral disorders, and 63% of teen suicides. These statistics, and many others like them, show that men must step up and do the job for their families. You, the single moms, need this. You deserve it and have a right to expect it. The men who fail to do it must learn the skills of parenting, and then actually perform them.

Some of you might not want to see those fathers again. That's understandable, and, in some cases, it's a sad truth that those fathers should not return. These are the men who have given up. When they did that they not only gave up on themselves, but they gave up on you and the children. They threw away their rights as fathers. Some might earn their way back, but we know that others won't.

There are many among us who have failed in the past, but who now want to step up. We want to join the ranks of responsible fathers everywhere, and do everything necessary to help you, the single moms of the world, and our children. We know we have a lot to answer for, and that we must earn the respect and love of our families. We will do it. That's an unbreakable promise, from us, to you, and to our children.

We give you our pledge that we will acknowledge our mistakes of the past, and take responsibility for the future. We will heal the hurts that we've caused, and protect you, and our children, from harm. We will work hard, and bring home our paychecks. We will take worries about money off your shoulders, paying our own way, while we ensure that our children are free from the shackles of poverty.

We will be full partners in creating the best homes for our children. We will set a good example, helping little boys grow up to be righteous men, and little girls to become good, compassionate women like yourselves. We will take an interest in our communities, through churches, schools, businesses, and civic organizations.

In the following chapters, we will go into the details of this pledge to you. We will look at the problem of absent fathers in more detail. We will show how fatherhood works in healthy homes, and how today's absent fathers can learn to become concerned, caring, and ever-present dads. We will also show alternatives to fatherhood—routes young men can take outside of parenthood, while still acting responsibly toward the children in their lives. We will help well-meaning young men turn their best intentions into everyday facts of life. The former lawbreaker can become a respected role model. The former drug abuser can teach a child to say no. The man who once lived a violent life can show the true value of peace and cooperation.

For some of us, this won't be easy, but we know that it must be done. Too many homes have been broken; too many women have cried; too many children have grown up amidst poverty, ignorance, and crime.

We know that if we do this sincerely, and invest our hearts and souls in the mission, our investment of work, effort, and love will come back to us many times over. There's no calculating the value of family. No ledger can show the love and dreams of a father when he's with his kids at the ballpark, or at church, or on Christmas morning. Statistics don't cover the pride a father takes in watching a young student getting that hard-earned diploma or the hope we feel when we watch our kids say their wedding vows.

Our hope is the future, our goal is love, and our dream is to help you, the single moms, make it happen. Fatherhood is the investment that never stops paying. If we do it right, it makes us rich from the start and keeps enriching our lives forever. Ours is an unbreakable promise to the single moms of the world: we will be there for you.

This letter is from all of us dads—those of us who are already there with you, and those of us who are coming home to make good on that unbreakable promise. This book is a guide for us all as we start this journey.

# THE SILENT CRY

C hildren don't always know what they have or don't have. A child is new to this world. The boy may know his home, the girl may be familiar with her family, but every day, children experience new wonders—things that we regard as normal but are like magic to them.

We often look at our children's discoveries in terms of our own lives. We give our son his first video game, thinking back to when we were young, and video games were something we only saw in arcades. We teach a child to use a tablet, recalling our first PC. When our parents gave us that PC, they were reminded of their family's first television, just as their parents remembered their first radio.

We recall those childhood moments because they made such an impression on us. To a child, it's all new—every birthday present, YouTube sensation, or smartphone. All the toys are new, but so is the world outside those toys—the real world that we adults have grown accustomed to. The little boy who learns how to play his new video game might be more concerned with the discoveries he's making on the baseball diamond for his Little League team. He might like sending an electronic image of a man into that batter's box on the screen, but the next morning he wakes up after dreaming of hitting his own home run in a real Major League stadium. The little girl loves her new tablet, but the first site she visits is the one that can tell her everything about the jewelry she'd like to wear with her new dress. Children enjoy the virtual world as much as the rest of us do, but their lives are here in the real world.

Every generation sees change, but children see more of it. Many of those changes are wonderful, but some look more like mortal threats. Most children long for things that are solid and dependable—things that won't go away. That's how they want their families to be, solid and dependable.

When a child is born into a caring family, the parents understand that it's up to them to give that child a good start in life. The child needs love, but security is almost as important. A child does best in a consistent atmosphere where he or she can grow and learn. Though a single mother might be able to create this environment on her own, she shouldn't have to. Almost any single mother will tell you that help is always welcome; oftentimes, it's a necessity. It's a man's job to give the mother of his children all the help he possibly can. He's there to make her job easier, and their children's lives better.

This is where many men fail. Some men fail to support their children financially. Others fail to take an interest in them. Some men run away. Others stay and set a bad example. Some fathers go to prison. Some abusive fathers who never have to face a court's judgment might be better off behind bars.

Men fail their families for many reasons, some intentional, some not. Some men are barely aware that they have families, or simply don't understand that they've created families. Some have no idea what "family" means. We've all seen the loudmouthed guy who has sex with every woman he can, and who seems to regard each neglected child he's produced as one more proof of his manhood. This is a man who has a lot to learn, but he's afraid to learn it. In truth, his children and his attitude are proofs that he's not yet truly a man. To become one, he would have to change, but that prospect scares him more than any other. He thinks of himself as free, but in truth, he spends every day retreating further and further into his prison of cowardice.

Most of us understand that neglecting a child is far from a badge of honor. It's a sin, a crime, and a reason to feel deep shame. The man who boasts about fathering children he's never seen or cared for is just admitting his fears. When this is pointed out, this cowardly father will claim ignorance ("I didn't even know she was pregnant..."), injustice ("When she was born they had me locked up on a trumped-up charge..."), or obstruction ("Her mama won't let me set foot in that house..."). It's the same old story: When a man fears his own shadow, someone else is always to blame.

The problem passes down from one generation to the next, almost as if it were a legacy. Many of these men grew up in homes without fathers. Often "home" was nothing more than a place to live that changed each month, almost like the weather. Most of these residences were depressingly similar: junk-food dregs in the kitchen, a lot of violence in the air, and the constant stench of cooking drugs. This kind of background doesn't justify their behavior, but it does explain some things. If you grow up in an atmosphere that doesn't even include the possibility of family, it's hard to understand what "family" is.

Some boys grow up like this but realize there's something missing. They look at the world around them and notice that other kids live in real families. They watch those kids go to school, work at jobs, and strive to do something with their lives. They recognize that most of these more successful kids have a mom and a dad at home, as well as love, direction, and stability. The neglected boys grow up to be men. Some of these men investigate themselves and find the courage to change. When they do, amazing things can happen. But they must take a look inside and find the courage. Otherwise, the cycle goes on and on.

Fatherhood brought the rap artist, 50 Cent, face-to-face with this problem. Curtis James Jackson III, who would become "50 Cent," was born in a tough part of Queens, NYC, called South Jamaica. By the time of his birth, his father was long gone. 50 Cent's mom wasn't too concerned about that. She was on her way to becoming a major drug dealer, a job that doesn't have any built-in maternity leave. After the birth of her son, she lived another eight years before an unknown assailant drugged her, closed the windows, turned on the gas, and left. Her murder was never solved.

Through those years, she had supported her son with her drug dealing. Her finances were erratic; sometimes there was plenty, while other times there was barely enough to feed her habit, much less her son. Her relationships were short-lived, some with men, some with women. There was no father in her son's life, and when she died, young Curtis had no real sense of what the purpose of a family might be. With his mother gone, the eight-year-old moved into the house of her parents. They had eight other children of their own living there. All were uncles and aunts of the future 50 Cent. Suddenly he'd gone from a day-to-day life without family, to a house so full of dysfunctional relatives that all he wanted to do was escape. His grandparents tried to supervise him, but they couldn't. He was just one of the many blips on their radar. By the time Curtis was twelve he was telling them of his participation in many after-school programs, but none of his stories were true. Instead, he was spending that time selling drugs. One might think of him as following in his mom's footsteps.

Curtis (who soon adopted the name "50 Cent") dealt drugs throughout his teens. During those years he was also boxing in gyms and starting his rap career, but drug dealing was his way of life. Then in 1994 he was arrested and did some time. The arrest and jail time didn't change his life much, but according to him, the birth of his first son, Marquise, did. That happened in 1997, two years after he got out. "When my son came into my life, my priorities changed, because I wanted to have the relationship with him that I didn't have with my father," 50 Cent later told an interviewer. He said the birth of Marquise caused him to quit dealing drugs and go into music full-time. But he kept up much of his "gangsta" lifestyle.

However sincere he may have been about changing his life, the result has been far from perfect. 50 Cent broke up with his son's mother not long after she gave birth. Three years later the rapper was shot nine times in the neighborhood where he'd grown up. The shooting was said to be the revenge of a drug lord who was unhappy about the lyrics in one of 50 Cent's early recordings. 50 Cent came back from the edge of death. Not long after he recovered, his music career took off.

Since then, 50 Cent has had relationships with various women. With one of them, he fathered another son. Born in 2012, this child is named Sire. Marquise's mother sued 50 Cent for lifetime support but lost. Nonetheless, Marquise finished high school, where he starred in basketball. He hoped to go on to a college career playing hoops, and then turn pro. Many felt that he simply wasn't talented enough to fulfill these ambitions but was trying to make it on his father's name and fame. Apparently, the college and pro scouts agreed. Like so many high school hopefuls, Marquise didn't receive any offers.

Has he really been trying to cash in on his dad's celebrity? With such frayed family connections, who would blame him? 50 Cent's net worth is said to be well over $100 million, but he's also flirted with bankruptcy. The entertainment world is full of fly-by-night fortunes. If Marquise wants to exploit his connection with his dad while it still has a value, that might be a smart business decision. Still, it's tragic when a father and son's only bond is money. It's no surprise that Marquise has described his relationship with his father as "strained."

The high stakes of finance and fame are the only real difference between 50 Cent's story and thousands of other cases of absentee fathers. In interviews, 50 Cent has little sympathy for his own biological father. He's never even seen the man. When interviewer Larry

King asked him if he wanted to meet his dad, 50 Cent said: "I have no interests in it. The mistakes I made early on, he could have been there to help me not make those mistakes."

In this comment, 50 Cent shows some real understanding of what's happened. His father didn't just walk out on 50 Cent's mom; he also abandoned her unborn son. This left 50 Cent to fend for himself in a world full of drugs, crime, and violence. Whatever ideas or opinions the child might have had about family would've been twisted by this.

50 Cent later learned that there was a different world out there, one of money, fame, and respect. He wanted to be a part of that world, and he also wanted to be there for his son. He got the money, fame, and respect, but Marquise has said his father wasn't there for him. The rapper had good intentions, but he had never learned any parenting skills. 50 Cent realized he couldn't turn his back on his son, but he didn't know how to be a real dad. No one had ever taught him. Will

Marquise overcome this, and learn to be a good father? Only time will tell.

This is a depressingly typical story, but it happened in atypical circumstances. Most fatherless homes don't produce a multimillionaire star. But 50 Cent is a part of four generations of dysfunctional families, and without help, more will follow. His grandparents had more children than they could handle. In their children's generation came the sad tragedy of his mother. We've seen 50 Cent's difficulties with fatherhood, and now his older son seems to be setting himself up for a fall.

One of the root causes of fatherless families is the cycle of poverty. Though 50 Cent broke this cycle, his grandparents, uncles, aunts, and his mother had been caught in its clutches throughout their lives. 50 Cent made a huge fortune, but the tragedy of absentee fathers has a momentum all its own. No amount of money can guarantee responsibility.

Money is not responsible; poverty is not responsible; statistics are not responsible. "Responsible" is something that only humans can be. The first rule of responsibility is that we must come face-to-face with our situations. For an absentee father, this means facing his family.

This is seldom easy. A returning father isn't always welcome, especially if he shows up at the door unannounced. Though some single mothers are happy to see their children's fathers come home, others would rather these absentee dads remain distant memories. When things don't work out with the men who father their children, many single moms move back home with their parents. These parents might regard the return of the father as a threat. He might be a drug user or a thief. He might be a parasite looking for others to support him.

If you are an absentee father, and you want to reenter your children's lives, you should understand that you're going to have to earn that privilege. That's the price you pay for leaving. If the children's mother is doing her job, and keeping what's left of the family together, then you must respect her decision. That means you must ask her what you can provide that she needs.

Sometimes a single mom doesn't even want to talk to an absentee dad—often with good reason. If you are a father in this situation, you must make amends. You must do this quietly, gently, and without disrupting her life, or the lives of the children. If she won't talk, instead of trying to pressure her, find other ways to communicate. One way to start is by sending her money. If you're behind in support payments, that's the best place to start. Pay until your debt is settled, and then continue paying whatever you owe. Write to the children's mother and tell her what you are doing and why. Assure her that you won't try to barge into their lives and take over. In these first contacts, you shouldn't ask for anything. Just tell her you're finally paying your debt.

Once you've established a regular and consistent record of paying what you should have paid before, then you can ask their mother about a possible contact. If she's willing to work with you on this, listen carefully to everything she has to say. If she's not willing, don't go running to a lawyer. Though you might have certain legal rights, you're still the one who left. Be patient. Continue paying the support you owe and restate your request with each payment. Don't demand or try to force things in any way. Be tactful, reasonable, and responsible. Assure her of your love for the children, and of your willingness to help them in any way you can. If she still doesn't listen, see if you can get someone you both trust to act as a go-between. Allow this person to state your case for you, then invite your children's mom to respond the same way. If you've waited, and tried these things, and nothing gets through, then, and only then, you might want to investigate legal remedies.

It's a demanding process that often requires a lot of patience. Understand this from the start, and make sure you're ready to wait if it takes time. If you lose your temper, you can easily destroy whatever chance you have. Just be the best man you can be, and don't let yourself slip—not even once.

Often a mother will respond to real evidence of reform, and an admission of guilt. The evidence should come first. That's why you should start paying what you owe before you approach the mother with any requests. If she sees that you're living up to your financial responsibilities on a dependable schedule, and then recognizes that you understand what you did wrong, she will have a moral obligation to respond. Often that's the key. Once you two are talking, you're beginning to share some of the aspects of parenthood. Eventually, this can lead an absentee father back into his children's lives.

What if such a scenario is unrealistic, or even impossible? You or your children and their mother may have moved. You might be in prison, or maybe you've achieved success and built a whole new life with another woman. How does an absentee father return when he's taken on the obligations of a new wife and family?

That's when you must focus on the main problem: responsibility. What are your responsibilities in this new life? How can you fulfill those, while accepting your obligations to the children you left behind? You must find an acceptable way to do that because that's a father's job.

Many absentee dads are in prison. Few of these prisoners can offer their children any financial support. Prison limits what you can provide, but you still have options. Begin with sincere efforts to reform. Be a model prisoner. Take courses, learn skills, and prepare yourself to succeed in the outside world. Tell your children's mother what you are doing. Show her that you are setting goals and reaching them. Write your children, and tell them about the mistakes you've made, and your efforts to redeem yourself. Admit what you've done (without getting graphic—remember you are saying this to children) and show them that real redemption is possible. To show that clearly, you must become living proof of it.

But what if you're in the opposite situation? What if you once made some mistakes, but now you're doing well? What if you have a good job and a loving family? All of this should be good, but if the children you left behind get none of the benefits, your success is far from complete.

A man who abandons one family, then lives up to his responsibilities with another one, is only doing half the job—and being half a man. The first mother and their children deserve better. If she's found another man, and he's accepted and fulfilled the role of father, then your financial duties aren't so great, but if she and your children are struggling, you must help.

This is when a father must listen. He must listen to the family he left behind, but he must also pay attention to the needs of his present family. This is difficult, to say the least, but many men have done it. If your finances won't cover the needs of two families, do all you can, and look for any help that's out there. Can you help the family you left to make the best use of public assistance? Can they qualify for food stamps? Education programs? Might their church help? Research these things and tell the children's mother what you find.

In any of these scenarios, you must start by taking the first step. If you have no job or money, the first step might be getting hired and receiving a paycheck. If you're doing well, you could begin with a check and a promise of regular support. If you are in prison, the first step would usually be to make contact. Call or write and put your commitment into words. Think about what you say. Don't make any promises you can't deliver on.

When you make progress in your efforts to change, don't expect congratulations. Remember, you are simply doing your duty, and repaying a debt you owe. The responsibilities you take on now were always there. You just weren't paying attention; now you are. The only return you should expect is the satisfaction you get from doing the right thing.

Any man can abandon his children, but deep inside, he will hear their silent cries. Many absentee fathers learn to ignore that cry and live their lives as if those kids weren't even there. This drains the manhood out of them. They might look like men, and sound like men, but at their cores, they are hollow.

If you are becoming, or have already become that empty man, there's still hope. Face the facts of what you've done. Look at the needs of your children and see what you can give them. Show them how to correct their mistakes by correcting your own errors. Confess, ask forgiveness, and offer them all the love and support you can. They may love you or ignore you for your efforts, but in the end, you will be a better man.

# Our Future, Their Tomorrow

L et's imagine a world without fathers or even the memory of the fathers who were once here.

A worldwide epidemic hits, striking down all the adult males on earth. Little boys are still here—all the male children below the age of ten. The epidemic doesn't touch them, nor does it afflict women or girls— except to erase all clear recollections of the men they'd known. They know men were there, as fathers, brothers, boyfriends, and husbands, but they can't remember what these men did or said. Their world is left without any full-grown males—no single men, nor any that are married. There are no grandfathers or fathers, or even men who have never had any interest in becoming parents.

For children growing up in this new world, it would be as if fatherhood itself had skipped a generation. There are no male doctors, lawyers, teachers, construction workers, athletes, or movie stars. No men are on TV or on the internet. All male priests and ministers are gone. Boys have no one to emulate. When girls look at boys, they can't imagine them as men. These girls have never seen a real live man. No one really knows what marriage is, and, for a while at least, the idea of the family must change.

This new world has a huge hole in it. With no men to teach them, the boys must learn a lot on their own. The world's mothers can feed, clothe, shelter, and even educate their young sons, but only up to a point.

Whatever these women say about what a man feels, sees, or thinks is pure imagination. In their minds, they will create the images of men as they want them to be, rather than what men really are.

Several months after the epidemic struck, a woman named Evelyn gave birth to twin boys. She named them Alan and Karl. Though she couldn't remember the man who'd gotten her pregnant, Evelyn knew she must raise these boys to be good husbands and fathers. She realized there would be no more fathers until her sons, and their whole generation, matured. But Evelyn had no idea what a good husband and father might be. Her attention had always been on her own desire to be a mom, and in this new world, real men weren't even a memory.

When she and her sons had just celebrated the boys' eleventh birthday, Evelyn asked her friend, Alice, "What would a good man be like?"

"A couple of good men would take a lot of the work off our shoulders," said Alice.

"What work would a good man do?"

"For one thing, a good man would take care of your sons."

"He would really do that? He would feed them? Teach them? Tell them what they can and can't do?"

"I think so. Wouldn't it be the man's job to look after the boys and our job to raise the girls? Aren't they supposed to be our partners? I think that's how it must've been before, though I don't really remember."

"That would make sense," said Evelyn. "Would he do anything else?"

Alice thought for a moment. "I'm sure he would. Right now, we do everything, don't we?"

Evelyn nodded. "Everything a child can't do."

"That's right. We go to work, come home, and take care of our kids. I think if we had men around, they would do all the housework while we would be out doing our jobs."

"They wouldn't have jobs?"

"I don't see why they would," Alice said. "Would you want to give up your job to a man?"

"Of course not," said Evelyn.

"Besides, they would have enough to do right here at home, wouldn't they? Just think: a man to do the dishes, mop the floors, get the groceries, cook the meals... a man to help the kids with their homework, and talk to their teachers... a man who would play with them, and teach them games. They would get the kids toys... maybe be handy enough to sew, or even build a nice dollhouse..."

"But that's a lot more than raising the boys," Evelyn said. "Now you've got men tending to our daughters, too... cleaning for them, cooking for them, teaching them. Would we do anything... I mean, anything at home?"

Alice laughed. "I guess we could come home from work, sit back, and put our feet up."

"That sounds nice," said Evelyn, "but I would miss a lot of that stuff, especially games, and helping with homework. How would I get to know my boys if I didn't do any of that?"

"Oh, I'm sure they'd come in and introduce themselves. We could just relax and enjoy them."

"And the men would do all those other things?"

"That's right. But we'd help a little with the girls. I don't want any daughter of mine being raised just by some man. Do you?"

"No," Evelyn said. "I don't think I would."

"Of course, you wouldn't. So, we would take them shopping for clothes, teach them about makeup, and maybe take them into where we work, and show them around."

"I guess that's how it was when there were men."

"I'm pretty sure that's right," said Alice. "What do you do with those boys of yours?"

"Just about everything. As your boys grow up, you'll see. They're not like us girls."

"From what I've seen, boys need a lot more attention than girls," Alice said. "More toys, more discipline, more direction. Do you think that's true?"

Evelyn sighed. "I guess so, but I think that's because they don't have any men around. I don't really know what men did—can't even recall what a full-grown man looks like, or how they smell or sound— but I'm pretty sure it would be easier if they were here."

"Your sons will be all grown up soon enough," said Alice.

"But I don't even know what that means," Evelyn fretted.

"Nothing we can do about it," Alice muttered with finality.

In that kind of world, these kinds of conversations would be common. Women would have many questions, but no answers. Children would have to reinvent men's roles in life. Adult women would control things, and, for a time, everything would be different.

Would it stay that way? It's unlikely. Everything changes over time. As these boys grew up, they would reinvent their roles. Biology would cast them as fathers, but their actions would define the real meaning of fatherhood.

Evelyn and Alice's ideas about men would probably prevail at first. Women would be in control so they would teach their boys cooking, cleaning, and sewing before they thought of taking the boys fishing or hunting. If there were ball games to take them to, the players would be women. They would want their boys to help them around the house and learn to do the grocery shopping. They would raise their little girls to go to work and be breadwinners.

But both sexes would know they were missing something. Women would want their men to be strong.

Women would also want more time with their kids and would demand that their men give it to them. Men would want to get out of the house. They would want to work and play. Their sons would want a parent who looked like them. They would respond to dads who were interested in sports, the outdoors, and competition.

Yet, if women controlled the whole adult world, even for one generation, some changes would become permanent. These women would teach their sons to respect women. They would expect their boys to wash some dishes, learn a few recipes, and vacuum the living room carpet. Most of all, they would want their sons to grow up to be good dads. Like Evelyn and Alice, none of these women would be sure what a good dad was. But they would be certain that it was a good father's job to share day-to-day responsibilities. They would want their men to be there for them, and to do whatever needed to be done.

Though this might sound far from reality, it's not so far-fetched. In the real world, communities are ravaged by the absence of fathers. So many fatherless children grow up in poverty. So many fatherless teens turn to crime and drugs. So many daughters of single moms become single moms themselves. Too many of these girls grow up without any knowledge of what a man's role is in a family. Their homes are run by mothers and grandmothers. The boys they know at school often don't attend. The boys they know on the street are often already on the wrong side of the law. When these girls look at their immature male counterparts, those are their first images of what men really are. They never get a fuller picture.

In some ways, Evelyn and Alice have it easier than these girls. In a world without men or even the memory of men, women see their duties clearly. They understand that their babies need care and that their children need guidance. They may not remember who men were, or what they did, but they know those men were supposed to be equally responsible for the children of this world. That knowledge alone will help them raise their boys to be fathers.

In neighborhoods where most fathers are absent, the women have a much harder job. Even when a father has fled, he still has a kind of presence, and it's seldom good. The possibility of his return always looms in the background. Many of these absentee dads do return for brief visits or even longer stays. When they do, they usually bring all their bad habits with them. This is when potentially good boys learn how to manufacture and sell drugs. It's also when girls sometimes get abused and molested.

Deadbeat dads who come home for a quick visit often leave their families poorer, sorrier, and less secure.

If you see yourself, or any part of yourself, in these descriptions, it's time to make some changes. That doesn't mean you have to start doing all the things women do. It means you must step up and do what a man does. This doesn't include violence, abuse, drugs, or crime. It does include work, patience, and empathy. If you're coming home from prison, this adaptation might be an even bigger problem. In addition to everything else, you must rise above your past. If you are putting a checkered past of crime, drugs, or abuse behind you, real contrition and apology will be necessary. You must be sincere.

None of this is simple or easy. Responsibility is hard work, but if you are a father, it's the work you need to do. The pay for doing it well is a lifetime of accomplishment and fulfillment. You are the one who provides job security. You do that by staying in your children's lives as a positive source of love, care, stability, and support. Your children need you; their mother needs you, and the rest of us need you. All you need to do is the hardest job of all: step up and do the right thing.

# No Higher Honor

We learn the Fifth Commandment as children: "Honor thy father and thy mother." When we are children, our Sunday school teacher gives it emphasis, saying: "When you girls and boys go home, remember to do what your parents tell you to do. It's in the Ten Commandments." The teacher is right about the meaning, but that's not spelled out in the language. If you look at those six words, not even one says anything about obedience, yet just about everyone from every faith has always interpreted the words of that commandment to mean that we should obey our parents. They are right. The ancient Hebrew word for "honor" implied obedience. But there was more to it than that.

When we honor someone, we hold that person up above the rest, recognizing his or her worth. We sometimes honor people for what they've done. We give Oscars to the best filmmakers, Pulitzers to the best authors, and Nobel Prizes to those who work for peace. We honor these people's talents and accomplishments. In the rare instance that someone's achievements are proved to be false, we withdraw these honors.

Honoring a parent is different. If you are the biological father of a child, no one can change that fact. You might walk away from the child, or a judge might strip you of your parental rights, but you are still the male who helped to create this little person. Does that mean your child must always obey you? No. If you order the child to violate other commandments, he or she has a duty to disobey you. Then the only honor the child owes you is to acknowledge that you are his or her dad—nothing more. The real honor of fatherhood must be earned.

Whether he knows it or not, a father who orders a child to do something truly wrong is taking a step away from his role as a father. He's removing honor from the equation and trying to replace it with raw power. He's abusing the parental privilege, and there's no reason to reward him. The closest a child can come to honoring such a parent is to say "no" politely.

Fatherhood is the greatest honor a man can have. Some men seem to come by it easily. A young man might marry a woman he truly loves, and when their children start arriving, he steps right into the role. It's as if it were made for him. He changes diapers, heats a bottle at feeding time, then, as the years pass, he helps with homework and gives good advice about life. When his children cause trouble, he's firm, but always fair. When they do the right thing, he encourages them. He likes being a dad and his children like him. Every one of us wants a dad like this, but only a few kids are that lucky.

This "perfect" dad isn't quite as perfect as he might seem. He's made mistakes, had a few accidents, and some of his decisions have flaws. But he likes being a father, and long before he ever got married, he developed the habits a good dad needs. He learned the value of patience, the necessity of honesty, and the difference between right and wrong.

But what about all the imperfect dads? What are they doing wrong? And how can they make it right?

A father's most important task is simply to be there. A father who leaves his family behind is no father at all.

Fatherhood is the highest honor any man can aspire to. It's not hard to reach the pinnacle where a man finds this honor. All you need to do is find a woman who's willing and physically able to bear children. If you can get her pregnant, she can give you kids, but that doesn't get you the true honor of fatherhood. That takes time, effort, and endurance. There are no shortcuts.

Many men flee from this highest honor. They know it involves huge responsibilities, and these men aren't ready to accept any obligations. They understand that claiming the honor of fatherhood and accepting its rights means contributing to the support of a child. That's a line they won't cross. If something involves consistent financial support and stable home life, these guys just aren't interested. They are just responsible enough to recognize their own weaknesses. Should they do more? Of course. Will they? Not likely. But at least they get out of the way.

When a truly irresponsible man—one who finds it impossible to believe in his own imperfections—claims the honor of fatherhood, he falls into a trap. He's got the commandment memorized and takes it literally. Such a man usually interprets the commandment's reference to "mother" as an indirect honor to him. He thinks all women should obey their men, and he assumes God believes that, too. This man takes it as gospel that any child of his must honor him in each way, forever and always.

The fact that he never honored his own father doesn't bother him. The fact that he doesn't honor anyone at all doesn't occur to him. In his mind, he created this baby. He sees the baby's mother as no more than a pipeline for his own genes. The woman is his; the baby is his, so he must deserve the honor. But the man who believes this never finds any honor at all. The best he will ever get from his family is fear, pitty, and grudging compliance. At worst, his family will turn on him, and he'll find himself abandoned, hurt, or in jail.

A good father earns the highest honor every day. He may work a job with long hours or have leisure hours to spare. He might be a member of just about any religion or political party. He might be a sports fan, or he might like the opera. Whoever and whatever he is, his first thoughts in the morning, and his last thoughts before sleep are about his kids.

Fatherhood is the job that keeps on giving—both ways. You give your kids love; they give it back to you. You don't need professional expertise or an advanced degree. The honor that goes with those is fine, but it's not the same as the reward that comes from being a good dad. A good dad receives his honor from his kids; he gets it every day. Sometimes they might not express it in words, but they give it. Some kids can't find the right words until long after Dad is gone. In a recent piece in The *Huffington Post*, Rashaan Chisolm wrote of her late father: "My dad drove the A-train, but to hear him speak you'd think he had a doctorate in linguistics... I want [people] in my life . . . who realize that worth doesn't come from where you grew up, how much money you had or where you went to school." Her dad wasn't there to read that, but there's no doubt that he died knowing that his daughter loved him.

In the Bible, we see many fathers, both good and bad. When Abraham and his wife, Sarah, experienced the despair of never having a child, God worked a miracle and gave the couple a son, Isaac. God waited until the boy was growing up to test Abraham's devotion. God then nearly destroyed Abraham by ordering the poor man to prepare to sacrifice Isaac. It becomes clear that this father will do God's bidding, but in doing it, he will be destroying himself. God doesn't intend for this to happen. When God is satisfied that Abraham is willing, but almost fatally saddened, God stops him, saving Isaac's life, and saving his bond with his father.

This is the first place in the Bible that explores the deep connection between fathers and children. Many others follow. Isaac goes on to marry and have twins: Esau and Jacob. Jacob becomes the father of twelve sons, and from them come the tribes of Israel. The relationship between Jesus and God the Father resolves itself in the Christian trinity, where the holy father, holy son, and holy spirit become one. All religions have stories like these to show the roles of fathers.

One mistake some irresponsible fathers make is to read more into these biblical stories than is there. Men read of "God the Father," and begin to think of the honor of their fatherhood as being connected to the Divine. It is, but not in the way they think. They see God as the all-powerful creator at the center of our universe. They conclude that this must mean that their family is their universe, with themselves at its center. These men begin to confuse the honor of fatherhood with the power that goes with it. They become versions of the irresponsible men discussed earlier in this chapter. They have what's called a "God complex." They don't understand that power always brings responsibilities. They think of their authority as absolute, and when someone in their family disputes them, they often get abusive. No family should allow this to happen. Violence has no place in a healthy family. When a father believes that might makes right, he has lost his honor.

***

We have noted that fatherhood is the highest honor a man can reach. Of course, for women, it's motherhood. But what goes into these honors? Why are they so great? Couldn't a man reach even higher stations? Couldn't a woman aspire to do much more than just take care of some kids?

We can set any goals we like, and, if they are within the realm of possibility, we can work hard, make the right moves, and reach them. A man might want to become the CEO of a huge company. A woman might strive to become an astronaut. These can be excellent and admirable goals. If these two get what they want, they're likely to make the news. The man will be famous for making a huge fortune, and for mastering the difficulties of the business world. The woman will set records for time spent in space, and she will perform scientific experiments that change the future of space exploration. They will become successes. Their colleagues will honor and respect them. In the larger world, these people will be known for these accomplishments, no matter what they do at home.

But these are two individual people. In the world of business, this man is one among many. He needs hundreds and thousands of people to work toward the same goals he has—or he must tailor his goals so people will follow him where he leads them. The woman who explores outer space is part of a similar effort: huge, diverse, and dependent on many people and systems.

But what if the man is a father? What if the woman has a husband and children waiting for her on the ground? These are the people whose honor is most important. These are the ones whose love is personal and real. These are the ones who should know them best, and who understand the true honor that these two people have earned. Maybe the astronaut/mother earns her honor even while she's hurtling through space. Once she's fulfilled her obligations as an astronaut, she might spend every free moment communicating with her husband and kids down below.

The CEO/father might do the same. Some top executives do. The late President Kennedy's dad ran businesses all over the country and made one of the world's biggest fortunes, yet he was more famous for his family, and the devotion he gave to his kids. He earned the love of his nine children. The elder Kennedy gave each child a million-dollar trust fund which the child received upon turning twenty-one. The elder Kennedy did this to give them the freedom to reject him if they wanted to. None of them even considered it. Their dad was a major part of their lives right up to his death. He knew what the highest honor was, and he worked for it. Not all business executives are so family-minded.

Our CEO might be a good dad, just as Kennedy was, or he might have the same attitude as the drug-dealing womanizer who doesn't even know which kids are his. He might practically live at the office and spend what leisure he has on vacations with mistresses. It's true that he's richer and more respectable than the drug dealer. His kids won't go to bed hungry or worry about college tuition. His wife and their children live in a big house and have the latest cars. But this man is never home—not even for holidays. His excuse? Usually, it's some variation of the following: "I want my kids to have every possible advantage—the best house, the best schools, the best health—all of it. That stuff costs money, so I need to make money. My wife stays home with our kids, so they get all the rest from her." He usually follows this by saying: "I'd love to spend more time with them, but I'm the breadwinner."

It's a thin excuse, and ultimately, it's a lie. A CEO who manages a huge company could find a way to get home at night. After all, some do. If his business is so dependent on what he does, then he could train others to do it, and make the time he needs. It's all a matter of priorities, and priorities are choices. This man chooses business over family. He might earn honor from the Business Council or the Chamber of Commerce, but he's not earning the highest honor of all. That would be waiting for him at home—if he would only go there.

Our CEO, and many other men like him, often fail to understand the honor of fatherhood. They know the world of competition and see each day as a battle. They fight for advantage and profit; some win, while others lose. They think of their families a little like a chess player might think of his king. Like the king on a chessboard, the family is something to be protected, sheltered, and preserved. Anyone who threatens it must be opposed and turned back. Anyone who provides it with benefits will receive proper rewards. The CEO moves his various pieces, buying this, selling that, while hiring and firing employees. With each move, he considers his family. Could it hurt them in any way? Is their income threatened? Might an action deplete their fortune? Will one move provide tuition at an Ivy League college? Will another move take that away?

This man is concerned only with the game of business. His thoughts are all about maneuvers, strategies, and gaining an advantage. But just as a chess player spends little time worrying about the heart and soul of his king, the CEO doesn't consider the details of his family. He would tell you that's his wife's job. If he makes money, and she mothers the kids, everything will be all right... right?

What this man is missing is that the honor of fatherhood is greatest when it's shared. That doesn't mean sharing the role with other fathers (though this sometimes happens). It means that fatherhood is a part of parenthood. It works best when motherhood is involved. This brings us back to that commandment again: "Honor thy father and thy mother." Children should honor each parent, but the greatest honor comes when children give it to both parents together.

The CEO needs to ask himself: How much is enough? When a man has a billion dollars, is it worth another million to miss his daughter's graduation? Does he need to buy that new company? Or would a long family vacation make more sense? Which meeting is more important: the one with the new client? Or the one with his son's math teacher? His new client will bring him more business. His son will bring him the future.

This is not to say that there's anything wrong with going all in on your business. We need companies to provide us with products and services. We need the jobs they create, and the opportunities they give us to fulfill ourselves.

But the essential part of most people's lives is in their families. Families give us our past, define our present, and fuel our hopes for generations yet unborn.

We need them. People who've lost their families tend to react by beginning to build new ones.

The single most essential male role in a family is that of a father. He may be the breadwinner, or perhaps he stays at home. He could have a fortune or make minimum wage. Maybe he can hit a baseball, or perhaps he's in a wheelchair. The main thing is that he be there and that he cares. A father who loves will be loved. A husband who honors his wife will earn honor from her, and from their children: the honor that's due to a good father.

That is the highest honor a man can receive.

# Five Habits of Highly Successful Dads

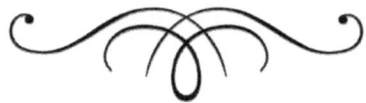

## *Five Habits of Highly Successful Dads*

Being a good father isn't always easy, especially at first, but it's something most men can master. Like any skill set, it relies on your self-discipline, and your ability to learn. You don't have to be a genius. All you need is the desire to improve, and a little sensitivity. With each aspect of fatherhood, you must look at the task, do it as well as you can, then do it again and again, correcting your mistakes. By the time you do it right, it will already be a habit.

Most good dads have good habits. Some of these habits are merely details, like getting up to drive the kids to school, or putting the bills in the right place so you won't forget to pay them. We might mention a few of these here, but our focus in this chapter is on the broader habits that help you deal with those details.

**Let's examine these one at a time:**

### 1. Quality Time

"Quality Time"—The phrase might sound like psychobabble from a '70s sensitivity class, but this term has real meaning, so you should pay attention. Some dads think they can solve the problem of being an absentee father by simply spending time in the same house with their kids.

Such a dad might feel good about himself because he stays home all weekend. On Saturday he eats lunch with his kids, then on Sunday, he accompanies them to church. He does that for several weekends. And it becomes a habit. That means the problem is solved, right? Wrong.

This dad has taken a short step in the right direction—then he stopped. Up until now, he's been an absentee dad, especially on the weekends. He was out with his friends from the time he got his paycheck on Friday, clear through to Monday morning. He went to bars with them, watched football, and they usually spent their Saturdays going on fishing trips where their bait never even got wet. Often, he never came home until it was time to go back to work on Monday morning.

Now he spends his weekends at home. What does he do there? He drinks beer, watches football, surfs the net, and spends his Saturday mornings making fishing lures that will never even get wet. He does have his Saturday lunch with his kids, but all he's willing to share with them is the sports section of the local newspaper. When his son asks for that, his father lets him have it. He hands his son the section, saying that it's good for a boy to read something that's "real paper and ink." Meanwhile, he picks up his own tablet and continues reading about his favorite teams online. He thinks of this as "real communication."

The Sunday trip to church is a good way for this dad to catch a quick nap. Then it's home for a day of football, basketball or baseball on the tube. His son comes in now and then to watch some of the action. Occasionally one of them might comment on a play, but otherwise, they don't talk much. The next time they see each other is when he drives the kids to school in the morning.

No matter how you cut it, this dad isn't giving his kids quality time. Quality time is the minutes, hours, and days that you spend with someone else. It's time that you truly share with them, in spirit, as well as location. There's nothing wrong with watching a few innings of a ball game together while saying almost nothing, but that alone is not quality time. Real quality time requires that you pay some attention to the other person's needs.

If this dad is making an effort to stay home, he should use that time to talk to his kids and see what they're doing and thinking. This might lead him to teach his son to tie those fishing lures—and maybe they'll even get them wet on a real fishing trip. If this dad is interested, he might encourage his son to try out for a sports team. He could start by taking him outside to play catch. He could teach his son how to hit a baseball, block a shot, or shoot a basket. At the same time, this dad could be teaching himself to be patient. These are the kinds of quality activities that go into quality time.

With a daughter, it's different, but the same principles apply. Learn about your daughter's interests. Even if these are totally feminine things, you can give her a male perspective. Some girls like sports and can share that with their dads. But a more traditional daughter might like only dolls, clothes, and worlds of imagination. In that case, get her to help you build, paint, and furnish a dollhouse for her dolls. Most girls like music and dancing. These activities are meant to be shared. Some fathers and daughters find common ground in the kitchen, cooking, and learning about food.

Quality time can be about almost anything. Sometimes it's just about talking. Many dads and their kids form a deep, lasting bond built on love, respect, and understanding, yet year after year, the only things they share are many heartfelt conversations.

The essence of quality time is a shared experience. This could be anything from having a leisurely breakfast together, to teaching your kids to drive. The main thing is to do these kinds of things on a regular basis so that they become habits—and always emphasize communication.

### 2. Do your best and lead by example.

The best way to be a good parent is by doing the right thing and doing the thing right. None of us are perfect about this, but we must try to be. When kids want to know how to act, they look at their parents. When they're with their friends, they might make fun of Mom and Dad, but whenever they want to do something grown-up, you are their model. That makes it even more important to do the right thing.

If a father is never there, his son will see that, and he'll learn that it's not important for a man to come home. He'll take this lesson with him into manhood. This absentee dad's daughter will grow up accepting the fact that men don't stay. When she grows up, she won't expect them to. These kids won't learn responsibility from you because they will never see you display it. Instead, they'll associate "home" with women, children, and work, while fun and pleasure will be forever linked with an escape from home and family. That's what you will be teaching them.

Kids learn to do what they see you do. Do you want your kids to go to church? Then you must go there. Do you want them to avoid alcohol, tobacco, and drugs? Then you must avoid those things. Do you want your children to be honest and truthful? Then you must tell the truth, and act with integrity.

This doesn't mean you have to be perfect all the time. No one is. When you make a mistake, admit it. Don't dwell on it or grovel. Simply state that you've made an error and that you intend to correct it, and/or avoid making it again. Show your kids that you're confident enough to admit it when you're wrong and strong enough to make things right.

A big part of leading by example is fairness. If you act fairly, your children will see that, and do the same. If you try to gain an unfair advantage or deny something to someone who has a right to it, don't be surprised if you see your kids doing the same thing.

Naturally, this has some limits. Adults and children live in different worlds with different rules. Children are more restricted. They don't yet know enough to make their own decisions, so we make most of those for them. It's our job to tell them what to do. As a child grows up, he or she learns more and more, gaining the ability to make his or her own choices. If we've set a good example, constantly making positive decisions, it's much more likely that our children will choose to do the right thing. Once again: the main thing we must do is to make it a habit.

3. **Demonstrate love and be brave enough to show your emotions.**

No father should be afraid to show his feelings. If you are happy, you should smile. If something's funny, you should laugh. Though few of us like to see men cry about little things, if sadness is deep enough, or the pain sharp enough, there's no reason a man shouldn't shed a tear.

Many men think that a man should be a rock, no matter what the circumstances. These men believe that any show of emotion is a sign of weakness. They believe women should be the only ones who show emotion. Most men who think this way also consider women to be weaker than men, not just physically, but also in their minds, hearts, and souls. They see women as inferior beings whose thoughts and feelings need not be taken seriously. The truth is, belief and faith in that kind of nonsense tend to make a man weak. A strong woman can dominate a man like that. He sets himself up for it.

Emotions are like breath and blood. They run through us. Controlling them is important, but a part of that control is recognizing that they are there and finding ways to let them run their course without causing damage to others. If you have anger, you must find some way to vent it. If you suffer a great loss, you must find a way to grieve. If you fall in love, you must find a way to say so.

A father must express love, hope, care, concern, pride, and even anger. He should search for ways to make these into positive forces in his children's lives. The best way to show this is to allow his children to see what he's feeling while shielding them from the passions they can't yet handle.

## 4. Develop a plan and invest in the future.

The thing to remember here is that your children are the future. You might have big plans, and you should make every effort to carry them out. But when you are older, and you are finishing your working life, what will be the result of all your efforts? That result will be obvious in the kids you raised — or abandoned.

This doesn't mean you should put your job before your family. You must balance these two sides of life, or, in some situations, combine them. But family should always be your main concern.

Your most important investment is the substance you put into the time you spend with your children. Unlike a house or a stock, whose value is measured in dollars and cents, this investment's value can't be expressed in numbers. A dad can spend two days with his kids and hardly notice them. Or he can spend an afternoon with them and make it into a time they will always remember. As we've noted before, you must be there... really be there!

When someone invests a large amount of money in a venture, they usually monitor it. A friend is starting a store, and you invest ten thousand dollars for a 10% share. Periodically you stop into the store and see how it's doing. If you never see any customers, you talk to your friend. If this shows up in the books in the form of losses, you talk to him again. If things don't improve, you demand action.

Kids are more important than that store. They outrank your investments, job, hobbies, friends, and all your other interests. Kids are your family. Even if you were to walk away, the connection would remain. If you make a fortune, they should be your biggest reason for doing it. If you already have a fortune, they are the best reason to maintain it.

You monitor the investment you put into your kids by investing more. You invest time in them so that you'll have more time with them. When they have kids, they'll want to do the same thing. When something goes wrong, you work with them to solve it. When something goes right, you show them how they capitalize on it and use it to their advantage.

You invest your hopes in your children. As you grow old, they will grow into maturity. They will start families of their own, giving you the opportunity to be a proud grandfather.

You invest love in your children. This is the biggest part of the future you're investing in. The love you give your children will come back many times over. It will give you so many other things: warmth, comfort, pride, and faith, to name just four. When you love and support your children throughout their youth, your investment pays dividends every day. As they grow up and go out on their own, you can relax a little, yet those dividends keep coming. If you make it a habit to invest in your children every day, you will ensure a bright future for yourself, and them.

### 5. Selflessness, and its companion... sacrifice.

When a father thinks only of himself, he might as well be absent. Selfishness and fatherhood don't go together. A father must train himself to always think of his children first. For some young men, this is easy. They have the right temperament, or they saw their own dads make it a habit to think about them. Whether you do this by nature, or you must teach yourself to do it, you must practice selflessness and sacrifice every day— fathers who don't aren't doing their jobs.

If this is difficult, train yourself to think of your children first at certain key times. Do it the moment you pour your morning coffee. Have they had breakfast? Is their homework finished? Do you need to drive them to school? Do it every time you get a paycheck. Look at the amount. Once the bills are paid, how much of that money will go to helping them, and how much will be spent on the things you want? Always be sure you take care of them first. This doesn't mean buying them anything they want. It means feeding, housing, and clothing them, and putting money aside for their future.

When you go into a mall or store to buy something for yourself, think of them. Will your purchase here limit what you can do for them? Is there anything here they need? Think of them every time you pass a church. Say a silent prayer for them. Help God grant any request you might have in your prayer by working to make it happen.

\*\*\*

These five habits are the foundation of successful fatherhood. A good father spends quality time, leading his children by setting a good example. He's not afraid to show his emotions or to invest in the future. He's selfless and willing to make any sacrifice if it helps his kids.

If you're just figuring out your approach to fatherhood, write down these five habits, then write three specific ways each habit can fit into your life. For instance: A father might lead by example by brushing his teeth in front of his son, eating all the food on his plate, and showing his wife the respect she deserves. At the end of each day, check off the habits you've followed and strengthened. Also, put a big mark next to any detail of any habit that you need to work on.

The principle behind all five is giving. If you learn to give of yourself, you will find that your kids give back far more than you could ever dream was possible.

# THE COST OF FATHERHOOD: A STATISTICAL PERSPECTIVE

G ood fathers make a difference. Most of us think that statement holds up even if we don't have right there at our fingertips the facts and figures that would prove it to be true. It seems so obvious: good fathers make a difference. It's one of those things we all believe, yet many of us have a hard time making it happen. Sometimes it's beyond our control. Some dads die young; sometimes, a mom walks out on a good dad, or the two can't get along, making divorce inevitable. More often, it's a choice. A father decides he doesn't want the responsibilities of fatherhood, so he walks away and never comes back. Often this is a man who would not be a good father anyway, but in most cases, that's a choice too. A man must choose to be a good dad; then he must follow up on his decision by doing the things a good dad does.

The numbers tell us that if a father is going to make a difference, he must be there. According to the U.S. Census Bureau, twenty-four million of America's children—one-in-three—live in homes where the biological fathers are gone. Most Americans agree that this is a crisis.

What does this absence do? We can start with dollars-and-cents. Absent dads leave their kids in poorer families. In 2011 a Census Bureau study gave the following figures about these children: They are four times more likely to fall below the poverty line. When a family has Dad at home, the kids have a seven in eight chance of escaping poverty. If Mom must go it alone, the family stands an almost even chance (44%) of being poor enough to need regular public assistance.

In 2007, researchers C. Osborne and Sara McLanahan studied mothers and their children between birth and when the children turned three. They found that, even at that young age, the children of single moms displayed more aggressive behavior than kids with both parents at home. This was especially true among boys. Studying data on over two thousand families, they found that a father's absence affected a child as much as any five partner changes would in the same three years.

The Infant Mortality Rate—the rate at which babies die in their first year of life— is one of the most important statistics in measuring the health and well-being of a nation's children. In the last two centuries, the drop in infant deaths has been dramatic throughout much of the world. Its single greatest effect has been on families and parenthood.

As infants have fared better, so have young children. Two hundred years ago, nearly half of the world's children died before their fifth birthdays. This still happens in many impoverished nations. But in the developed world, medical science has guaranteed that almost all infants survive into adulthood. Yet this rarity of infant deaths makes their occurrence even more traumatic. The loss of an infant has become a tragedy that ripples through families and communities. In 1998, researchers T.J. Matthews, Sally C. Curtain, and Marian F. McDorman studied infant mortality in the U.S.A. and found the rate was 1.8 times higher for infants of unmarried mothers than for married mothers. Why? No precise reason can be identified, but it is clear that Dad's presence makes a positive difference even when a life is on the line.

The difference that saves the infant's life might keep him out of jail when he's reached adulthood. In a 2004 study, "Father Absence and Youth Incarceration," the above-mentioned Ms. McLanahan, and another of her colleagues, Cynthia C. Harper, found higher rates of incarceration among males raised in fatherless households. The highest rates were among males who'd never had a father living at home at any time in their lives. So, the more Dad is there, the less chance his sons will see the inside of a prison cell.

Most of us have seen this in our own neighborhoods, and even our own families. A mother raises her children alone. As her sons grow older, she finds it more and more difficult to control them. They have no role models in their family, so they look elsewhere. The most obvious role models available are the flashiest men in the neighborhood—the ones with great clothes, expensive cars, and plenty of bling. Those kinds of things make a huge impression on boys just reaching their teens. These men are usually gang leaders or drug lords. The boys (who are quickly growing up into young men) try drugs, join gangs, and imitate the men they admire. By the time these young men turn eighteen, they are already in conflict with the law. Many have had brushes with the police, and some of them have already been to juvie. To these young men, a jail cell is just another address, similar to a bed in a barracks, or a particularly tough dorm. When they go to jail, they often leave pregnant girlfriends or single mothers on the outside. These young women must fend for themselves, starting the cycle all over again.

A good father would make a difference. What difference would he make? According to the National Responsible Fatherhood Clearinghouse's website (https://www.fatherhood.gov/content/dad-stats): "When fathers are involved in the lives of their children, especially [in] their education, their children learn more, perform better in school, and exhibit healthier behavior." The site also tells us that children from families with fathers at home have less disciplinary problems and perform better on tests of math and verbal skills.

Of course, "fatherless" is a relative term in all these studies. Not all single-parent households are entirely fatherless. About one in seven, or 14% of these households, are headed by a father. In the 86% headed by women, some have a father nearby. Still, two in five children in fatherless households haven't seen their dads in at least a year. Fifty percent of fatherless-household kids have never set foot in their father's house. That's not surprising when you consider that one in four of these absentee dads lives in another state. So, in most fatherless homes, the father is seldom or never seen. This encourages the same behavior in their sons as they get older while producing lowered expectations about men among their daughters for the rest of their lives.

So, what's the cost to the rest of us? This is where the numbers can't fully express the truth. What does it cost us when millions of children don't have a dad to help them with homework? Most studies show that fathers who stay with their families get much more interested in their kids' educations, especially in the later grades. These dads give their kids more focus and direction, encouraging them to go to college, and even graduate school.

Dads are a key component in efforts to solve the problems of incarceration and correction. Dads who stay with their families keep their kids from getting involved with gangs and drugs, which helps the kids avoid jail. Every year a man spends in jail costs the rest of us between $150,000 and $200,000. When you think of all the kids, and all the years this could add up to, it's easy to see that the dads who stay earn a vote of thanks from all of us—just for doing their jobs.

Dads who stay keep their kids off food stamps and other sources of public assistance. This helps these overstretched, underfunded programs target those folks who need them most: people whose limitations, handicaps, and disabilities leave them unable to work. If every dad stayed and fulfilled his responsibilities, public assistance could be redesigned to benefit the neediest—and the cost to the taxpayers would decrease tremendously.

Dads who stay help their families gain more stable living situations. Often a working dad is the difference between a real home and subsidized housing. With Dad's contributions, the family can often afford to buy a house. If the family is healthy and reasonably happy, a house can become a refuge from bad influences, as well as a place for love, learning, and planning. Families without dads are far more likely to need assistance with rent. They move a lot, creating instability. This only makes things worse for a family that's already on edge.

Dads who stay help their kids live healthier lives. Though Mom is traditionally more concerned with most family health choices, a good dad pays attention to this, too. He can help the kids through illnesses, make them healthy meals, and set a good example for a healthy life. He can reinforce Mom's health decisions, and help children accept doctor visits, medicines, therapies, and other health-related chores and limitations. And, of course, a good dad helps Mom pay the health bills. Though health care is now seen as a right, many health choices still have a price tag. Insurance, co-pays, and over-the-counter meds can all add up. A single mom gets swamped with so many bills. Dad can help with that extra paycheck, which is often larger than hers.

Dads who stay are available to their kids throughout their lives. They help their young children through school and help them stay in school longer. They keep their kids healthy and sometimes come to the rescue when financial problems arise. Their kids grow up to get better jobs and raise healthy families of their own. As we've already seen, these families are more likely to have dads who stay—which creates the cycle we need to keep our families healthy, happy, and prosperous.

# FATHER TO THE FATHERLESS: A FAITH PERSPECTIVE

*"He who fears the Lord has a secure fortress,*
*and for his children, it will be a refuge."*
Proverbs 14:26

God is a father to us all. In our world, a good father remembers that. When things go wrong, a good father falls back on his faith in the Almighty. When his children are in need, this father does all he can, then prays to God, and listens for the answer.

When a man becomes a father, he takes on new responsibilities. Some of these are obvious. He must support his children financially, feeding and clothing them, and giving them a home. As they grow up, he must see to it that they learn to support themselves and their own families. When they are small, he must protect them from bad influences. As they get older, he must teach them morals, ethics, and values.

As his children reach school age, a good father helps them with their schoolwork. He encourages them to do their best. If his son plays in Little League, the good father cheers him on. When the coach teaches these boys teamwork and fair play, their fathers should reinforce that by requiring those things at home. A good father teaches his children how to be good family members. A good father doesn't demand any special treatment for his children. He wants them to make it on their own merits.

When his children are still infants, a good father's connection with them is direct and inescapable. He does many of the things their mom does, and some things only he can do. Often, he will feed them, dress them, and tuck them in at night, just as their mother does. As they grow older, he might drive them places, and when they get old enough, he might teach them how to drive themselves.

As his children take their first steps into the outside world, a father's duties change. This is when his kids start playing with other kids, beyond the family, or block, or even the neighborhood. This is also when they interact with a much broader range of grown-ups. Once a toddler steps onto a playground, he or she begins making personal choices. Will he decide to climb that ladder to the top of the sliding board? Will she play with those kids in the sandbox? Or will it be the monkey bars? Which playmates will become their friends, and which ones will they learn to avoid?

These choices are bound to go in unpredictable directions. A father might look at his son and see an athlete, but the boy might decide he likes the library better than the playing field. Maybe the father thinks his pretty daughter is smart enough to become a teacher, but she decides to take advantage of her good looks and go to modeling school. A good father advises, and gives guidance, but knows when to back off and let his child decide.

All of these phases and choices involve other people. The infant sees dad and mom as the center of a tiny world. They provide, instruct, and set an example. But once the child starts playing with other children, everything changes. All those kids have fathers, as well as mothers, aunts, uncles, and grandparents. As the kids intermingle, the families follow. Dads get to know other dads through their kids. They go to PTA meetings and meet their children's teachers and the parents of their children's classmates. This is when children expand the worlds of their parents.

As parents begin comparing notes with these other grown-ups, dads begin to realize that their kids aren't entirely theirs anymore. This is when both Dad and Mom discover that they've given up a little of their authority. Some of that guiding power and authority has been transferred to all these other adults. Teachers, counselors, coaches, and other parents are taking their places in the children's world. Even more important is the fact that these children are beginning to make real decisions for themselves. These aren't just choices about playing and toys. A child in school makes choices about behavior, study, and after-school activities. These choices have the potential to shape a child's entire life.

The child's teachers decide what whole classrooms full of kids will do each day. They teach a child to read, write, and do arithmetic. As the child learns to do these things, a new universe of ideas opens up. The child uses this new knowledge to make even better choices with even greater effects on his or her future.

A well-known African proverb says: "It takes a village to raise a child." What is true in Africa is true here, and everywhere else in the world. As soon as a child can walk, he toddles away from his dad and mom. This doesn't mean he's rejecting them. He's just finding his place in life. That's when the rest of the world begins to rule his choices. At first, that world is no bigger than a village, but it quickly expands to include much more.

A good father will soon notice that the village proverb takes on a special meaning when it comes to children without fathers. As his children begin to play with children of other families, he'll realize that many of their moms are doing all the parenting themselves. He'll see young boys who appear to be missing something. This doesn't mean they are bad boys. Some of them might become his son's best friends, and one might even marry his daughter. But they have different needs and know different things, all because something vital is absent.

This lack might not be immediately obvious, but if he watches closely, he will notice signs. Some of these boys are more responsible, while others are looking for trouble. If one of them leads his own son into mischief, he might talk to the boy's mother, and discover there's no father at home. Or his daughter might have friends who don't seem to understand a man's role in a household. They respond negatively to any limitations he imposes. They see him more like a visitor and don't understand how he could have any authority. They only know about men who don't stay.

This is when a father must learn what it means to be a father to the fatherless. What does a good father do when he sees kids failing because they have no father? This becomes an important issue when these children of absentee dads begin interacting with his own kids. It might be on a playground, or on the street, or in his home. His kids' friends act up, he corrects them, and their initial reaction is to ignore him as if he was just one more piece of furniture.

In today's world, a young father might think twice before involving himself with children who aren't his own. Many parents, including single moms, don't like other parents to give their kids direction. Some moms are suspicious of all dads. They may have had bad experiences with irresponsible men imposing their authority in a household. They may know of cases of abuse, and, understandably, want to shield their children from harm. But if a child is in your home, or has no parent present, you are the adult in charge. If the visiting kids are well-behaved, there's no need to emphasize this fact, but when they start causing trouble, a father must be firm. Kids really want that firmness. Though many of them don't consciously realize it, they yearn for real direction. Gentle but consistent discipline helps them find it.

Most fatherless children want to have a dad. When they see other kids with dads, they feel envy and sadness. In an essay posted at fathers.com, a boy in the sixth grade writes:

I don't have a dad, but I want one. If I had a dad, I would feel like the luckiest kid in the whole wide world. A dad . . . would give you hope for challenges in your life, and if you're lucky, he will give you help on your homework. It's just too bad that I don't have a dad.

At the same site, a fatherless daughter in the eleventh grade tells us:

My father left when I was two, and I haven't seen him since. I don't know what it is to have a father. I see people who have one, and I wish I had mine. I've always wanted to feel the love of a father . . . I feel empty inside.

Both young people show the deep need every child has for a good father. Mom is great, and many single moms are true heroes. They understand what their kids are missing and do their best to find ways to fill the gaps left by the absent dad. But a great single mom knows that she can't do it all. When her son needs guidance, she can give it, but she understands that it's not quite the same as the "man-to-man" communication he would have with his dad. When her daughter wants support, this mom can give it, but sometimes she knows she's only a substitute for the father her girl really longs for. A good father is a living lesson, teaching his daughter what kind of qualities she will need when she looks for a husband.

Some single moms will seek out men to help them with their kids. Naturally, many of them look for possible husbands and fathers, but that's not always the case. A single mom might talk to other fathers in her neighborhood, or fathers of the kids at her children's school, hoping for a helping hand. She might look to the minister at her church or an admired teacher. Often this mom is too busy with work and keeping her household together and can't find the time to start a relationship with a potential husband and father. All she wants is a positive, meaningful male presence in her children's lives. This might come from one man or several, but whatever the source, or sources, she knows that her kids badly need this.

When a man becomes involved with fatherless children, he should always be aware of his role. Each case is individual, but some common principles apply. The first is to go slowly. As an adult, you are an authority figure, but you must always realize that a child's mother (or any other adult relative) outranks you. The child knows this, so you better be aware of it, too. In early encounters with a fatherless child, you should only assert your authority in rare situations. If you're left alone with the child, you're in charge, but you must also consider your duty to the mother. If you know her well enough, try to follow her rules. If not, your approach should be firm, but not overbearing. Learn what the child likes and try to make the experience fun. Kids like to test borders. They often aren't aware of what's appropriate and what's not. They've learned that one way to find out is to do whatever they want to do and see how adults react. It's your job to watch for these problems so you can teach children how to avoid them in the future.

If a child acts up, always remain calm. As noted above, most children want stability and direction. Often when they misbehave, they're simply frustrated by the lack of these things. Don't raise your voice any more than you must. Keep your tone even and confident. A child will often react to an adult's confusion by acting up more. If this happens, be decisive. Remove the child from the situation and make them take a time-out.

Be honest with a child. This doesn't mean you have to tell them everything that's on your mind. It just means that you should always be truthful with them about the things that matter. If the subject is something that's inappropriate to talk to them about, just say so in a straightforward manner, and move the conversation into another area.

As you get to know both mother and child, treat it as a learning experience. If this mom truly cares for her children, you should not do anything that might appear to threaten their relationship. At the same time, don't be afraid to deal with situations where exerting authority is the right thing to do. If the child gets into a fight or begins to harm or destroy something, you don't have to hang back. If the child is about to cause self-inflicted harm, obviously you must prevent it. If a child is doing something that we all accept as wrong, but his or her mom does nothing about it, stopping the child becomes a necessity. Do so in a way that brings the child's mom into the situation as quickly as possible. Make it clear that you aren't trying to take any of her authority away. You are only acting as her agent, and once she's in control, she is the boss. This will only change if your relationship deepens and you become the child's primary father figure.

In these kinds of circumstances, your true role is that of a concerned member of the community. If it takes a village to raise a child, you are simply a responsible citizen of the village doing your job. An essential part of that job is allowing Mom to step in.

But these are also the kinds of situations where a man is taking on a father's role. Correcting a child is something every dad must do. It's a learning experience for both of you. As you teach the child the basic rules of society, you are learning about the child — and often about yourself as well.

These are incidents that arise in everyday life. They are unplanned and unscripted. But if a man without children wants to learn more about how he might be as a father, most communities offer opportunities for that. You can volunteer to help in youth programs at your church or community center. You might teach Sunday school, or help coach a beginner's basketball or baseball team.

These kinds of programs bring you into contact with kids, and their parents. Look at the dads you meet. Which ones seem to do best with their kids? Watch them, ask them questions about parenting, and learn from them.

Fathering the fatherless isn't just for men who don't yet have children of their own. It's a task that begins with those men who are already fathers. Once a father lets his child begin to play with children from other families, he takes on the responsibilities of a more communal kind of fatherhood. He is still the primary father figure with his own kids, but he must watch over his children's playmates, and see that no harm comes to them.

In community settings, often there's more than one father present. This is when men must learn to share the duties of fatherhood. This isn't always easy. Every dad has a different approach. Some fathers might be more strict with their kids, while others might feel they can allow their children to make their own mistakes and learn from them.

A few fathers might be bad apples. Now and then an absentee dad returns home, bringing all his problems with him. He might be a drug user, or an aging gang member, who is simply taking a break from his sad street life. Some deadbeat dads come home, and suddenly get concerned about directing their children's lives. They have a dim understanding that they shouldn't have been gone, and now they want to make up for it all at once. They're determined to show that they're the best dads around, but they're usually the worst.

If you're in a situation with many dads, it's best to cooperate with the responsible men and neutralize the offenders. Dads who are on edge between a settled household and street life usually either learn to take responsibility or leave when responsible behavior becomes a big issue—dads who know what they're doing stick around year after year. If you are just beginning to learn the duties of fatherhood, stick with the ones who stay. They will teach you.

*"Children are a gift from the Lord; they are a reward from him. Children born to a young man are like arrows in a warrior's hands. How joyful is the man whose quiver is full of them!"*

*Psalm 127:3-4*

One of the best settings for learning about fatherhood is a church. Churches are our link with God, the father of us all. In a religious setting, a just and good father prays and gains spiritual strength. It comes from the Almighty, and from all those people who gather there to worship. Whether the minister has a family or not, he should have training in some aspects of fatherhood. A good minister will give guidance to the men in his congregation, helping them through rough patches with strength, wisdom, love, and faith.

Most of us try to be on our best behavior in church. Some immature minds see this as being hypocritical, but usually, that's not true. When we enter a church, we're visiting the earthly house of God. Why wouldn't we watch what we do and say more closely in that sacred place? In the church, families aspire to be the ideal version of themselves. In this setting, all parents keep a close eye on their children, teaching them respect for God, and all that he has created.

Though absentee dads might come home to rest up, they seldom spend their Sundays worshipping. When one does, he tends to control himself and try to be like the people around him. If he's an abuser, the abuse stops before he reaches the doors to the church. If he's an addict, he leaves his habit outside. Most churches have that effect on people.

We've already mentioned Sunday school, but churches offer many other opportunities connected with fatherhood. Most churches have youth activities throughout the week and on the weekends.

Another place to find activities connected with fathers is in schools. If you are already a father, and you aren't actively involved in your child's education, this is the place to start. Go to the PTA meetings. Get involved with some of the school activities aimed at dads and children. If your child's class has a Parents' Day, participate. You might have a lot of fun.

If you aren't yet a father, your local school is still a good source for volunteering opportunities. Do you have a skill that kids might be interested in? See if the school has a learning program where that skill might fit in a classroom setting. If not, then just bring your energy, enthusiasm, and commitment. Every school has opportunities for those qualities.

Fatherhood starts with your commitment as an individual, but that's just the beginning of a much longer process. A dad immediately shares this commitment with Mom, and sometimes with extended family. Beyond that, fatherhood is a shared experience throughout your community. You are your child's father, but to all those other children, you must act like a responsible father figure. When all the men do that, the community is always made better by their efforts.

All men should realize their own parenting duties don't end with their own children. All parents are responsible for the next generation. That's why it's so important to get involved in churches, schools, and other community activities that include parents and children. This involvement is important for dads who stay, and for men who want to be fathers. It's even important for men who have no intention of being fathers. We will look at that in Chapter Nine, but first, let's look at what goes into the choice of whether to be a father.

# DECIDING TO BE DAD

If it takes a village to raise a child, then virtually all the men who live there must be involved in the effort. To avoid this responsibility, a man would have to avoid all children. Though that might be physically possible, few men want to isolate themselves so completely that they would never see a child.

Most men want to be fathers. This desire might not seem like an overwhelming passion dictating every choice in every man's life, but for most men, it is a very basic urge. It's there in the man who is faithfully married and raises a house full of kids. It's also there in the deadbeat dad who boasts of all the women who've given birth to his children—children he will never know. Both men want to be fathers, but only the first one knows how to do it well.

A biologist might tell us that a man's desire to father children is simply an expression of our species' need to survive. Scientists can demonstrate that genes and hormones drive the human male to find a female who will have their baby. From this viewpoint, we are simply animals ruled by our instincts. But if that were true, we wouldn't have developed neighborhoods, communities, villages, schools, churches, or any of the other advances in human culture.

Researchers for the U.S. Department of Health and Human Services have found that 84% of men (five out of six) over the age of forty-five have fathered at least one child. As we've noted before, some of these men never know their children. A few might not even be aware that they have children. But five out of six of us do become biological fathers. That leaves millions of men who don't, and we will get to them soon.

Fathering and raising children is the most important thing a man can do. Often the whole process begins with no rhyme or reason. Unplanned pregnancies happen all the time. There are no exact figures, but most surveys indicate that about half of all pregnancies are unexpected. Some couples prefer it that way, and some religions encourage it. Couples who avoid birth control are inviting surprises. Many of them are aware of the risks and are glad to take their chances. They want children. However, many unplanned babies arrive to find parents who aren't prepared for them. Their moms didn't ask for them, and their dads don't really want to hear about them. These new parents aren't ready. Some of them will never be ready.

A responsible young man will ask himself: Should I be a dad? There might be several answers. He might say yes or no, or he might say "maybe." Both "yes" and "maybe" might be joined by "later."

Men decide to become fathers for a variety of reasons. Many men want sons to carry on after them. This might be the desire to see their family name endure, or to have another male to follow in dad's footsteps in a profession or business. Some men want daughters. They have a profound connection with women and want more girls in the house.

Some men don't care what the baby's sex is. They don't worry about its hair, eye color, or what it looks like. If the baby is healthy and has all the basic parts, these men are happy. These are the guys who are born to be dads, just as some women are born to be moms.

Even when these future fathers are growing up, they demonstrate patience, common sense, responsibility, and a strong sense of family. These men are the ones who study hard in school, find stable jobs, marry young, and the babies usually start coming right away. As their children grow up, these men never have doubts about their goals. They might have different skills, and try different parenting methods, but they all have the same aim: They want to raise their children to be all that they can be. These dads know better than to expect their kids to be saints and geniuses; they'll settle for decency and common sense. What these good parents want more than anything else is to raise their kids to be responsible citizens and good parents.

But often it isn't that clear.

Most men don't think about children and family in quite the same way women do. Women see families as having many of the qualities of nests. To them, the idea of family is one of warmth, love, support, and nurture. Most men appreciate those things, but a man usually sees his family as a road into the future. A woman's first instinct is to hold a child to her breast. A man is more likely to help a son or daughter stand up and face the world. Neither of these tendencies is exclusive to either sex, but understanding them helps us see how families work.

So, what happens when a boy grows up to be a man and is confronted with choices about fatherhood?

Should he feel he must be a father? Does he have to be a father to be a real man?

We live in a society that defines manhood in many ways, but fatherhood usually plays a role in any definition. One way to see this is in how we choose our leaders. What kind of men do we elect to public office? Are they fathers? Barack Obama is a father, as was every president since 1923. One of the few presidents who wasn't a biological father was George Washington, but this "father of his country" adopted his wife's children from her previous marriage and helped raise two of her grandchildren in their home. Most male governors, senators, and representatives have children. Voters see fatherhood as a badge of responsibility. If a man hasn't raised a family, we wonder about him. (As the number of women office-holders has increased, the same has been true of them: Most are mothers.)

We find images of fathers throughout our media. Back at the dawn of network television, one of the most successful shows was a sitcom called *Father Knows Best*. That set the tone for TV dads right up to the present. All these influences cause most young men to think that they really ought to be fathers. But is it true?

In many cases, the answer is "yes," but not always. Every man is different. Some men aren't ready for fatherhood. Some will never be ready. Some shouldn't become fathers now but might be ready later.

In a perfect world, each man would think carefully about the prospect of fatherhood, and then decide whether it's for him. He would consider the pros and cons, take a good hard look at his talents and resources, and make an informed decision. But we live in a messy world where this kind of clarifying moment is almost impossible to achieve. Many men never see it coming.

If you are suddenly, and unexpectedly, thrust into the role of being a father, you must face up to your responsibilities and do the best you can. But if you aren't yet a father, you can look at the issues, and set a direction for yourself. If you decide you want to be a dad, you can start preparing. If you choose not to, you can take precautions to see that you don't unintentionally stumble into fatherhood.

When a young man confronts the issue of fatherhood, inevitably he comes up against the question: What kind of man am I? Am I a good man? Am I honest? Confident? Smart? Talented? Am I patient? Do I like my friends' children? Can I talk to them? Do children interest me? Do I want to commit decades of my life to raise them?

If you're thinking about becoming a father, but you don't really like kids, you should think again. No man is required to become a father. Some men should never have kids. If this is you, don't worry. There's nothing wrong with feeling this way. Some of us leave childhood behind and live the rest of our lives in a world of adults. Many of these people are dedicated to their work. Some artists are like this. They might want to observe the world of children, but they have no compelling urge to participate in it. If you are one of these people, the key is to recognize it and do all that's necessary to avoid becoming a father.

If you don't think you want children, but you're not sure, it might be a matter of timing. We've mentioned men who seem to be born to be dads. For them, there's always no time like the present. If such a man can find a woman he loves, and she loves him, they might as well start having kids immediately. But these aren't the only good dads.

Most men probably shouldn't have kids too quickly. Ideally, a man shouldn't become a dad until he's married, and a man shouldn't marry until he's ready to settle down. When a man marries, he should be faithful. Life is full of temptations, and many young men will accept and give into some of these whims whether they're married or not. If you don't yet have the discipline to control your urges, you should wait before becoming a parent. Most young men aren't settled financially. A new father doesn't have to have a six-figure salary, but he should be able to support a child. Children are an expensive proposition. Most young men just entering the job market would do well to wait.

Waiting isn't easy, and young men are often impatient. In many jobs and businesses, this isn't a bad thing. An ambitious young man can use impatience like fuel, and it can help him earn raises and promotions. Many young entrepreneurs are impatient for success, which helps them start fast-growing profitable companies. But impatience seldom helps a man in his quest to be a good dad. Children grow and mature slowly. You might dream of your son becoming a great athlete or be confident that your daughter has the brains to be a CEO. But nothing happens overnight. Besides, when they grow up, they might have their own ideas.

A father needs to take a deep breath and concentrate on the present. A lot of years separate that little child from the mature adult he or she will become. You must help her with dozens of homework assignments before she can get an "A." You must watch your boy strike out a lot before he hits that first home run. In either case, patience is the name of the game. Any man who ignores that is setting himself up for disappointment.

Fatherhood isn't just a role you play. It's a life you lead, and a person you become. It will change you in ways you can't imagine. If it doesn't, you're probably missing something.

Up to here, we've been talking about fatherhood and you, but fatherhood's focus isn't you at all. It's about the kids. A father might dream of his boy becoming a billionaire, or his daughter being elected president, but as they grow up, he should learn to set his dreams aside and listen to their dreams. That boy might decide to become a minister, or Daddy's little girl might grow up and choose to become a housewife, giving him and her mom a bunch of grandchildren. A good father wants his kids to be all that they can be, but he knows he can't make all their choices for them.

Fatherhood is also about moms. Even when Dad is there, Mom still does most of the work. These two people make love, and she gets pregnant. She endures the morning sickness and goes to all those doctor appointments. She gets tests, and her body changes. She starts manufacturing loads of hormones, which affect everything from her appetite to her sleep schedule. She gains weight, feels unattractive, and goes on an emotional roller coaster. Finally, she has incredible pain that lasts for many hours—sometimes days, or even worse. Though modern medicine greatly reduces the dangers, what she's doing is still risky. It was not so long ago that childbirth killed more women than any other cause. Modern medicine has helped, but nothing is foolproof.

It's a father's job to do all he can to help her through it. That doesn't mean he must be there every minute, but he needs to be available, caring, and sensible. Often, he must be patient, even when she has a midnight craving for a banana split. He must listen to her, and respond, making sure she gets what she needs, and protecting her from harm. Sometimes he must remind her of the baby's needs. Other times he should be willing to take instructions.

He should talk with her doctor, and any other healthcare providers, listening to their information, advice, and directives. When the day arrives and she goes into labor, he should be prepared, alert, and ready to get her to the hospital. If all goes well, and they return home with a healthy baby, then the work really begins. A father must be willing to heat bottles, change diapers, and do all the little things that go with caring for an infant. This doesn't mean he does all the work. Most moms won't let him do even half of it. But a conscientious dad is as ready for fatherhood as a mom is for motherhood.

Though many young men rise to the task, this isn't a job for a teenager. A dad under twenty is often more child than man. He might work hard at it, and do it well, but a teenager shouldn't have to. He should be able to look forward to fatherhood as one of the rewards of experience and maturity.

Some men are ready to have kids when they are in their twenties, but many need even more time. Some will never be ready. Just as many smart, strong, and decent men choose to live this life, other equally smart, strong, and decent men decide not to. Often it seems as if our society demands that every male find a mate and start producing children. We've all heard the often-misused Biblical dictum: "Be fruitful and multiply" (Genesis 1:28). Teachers, ministers, politicians, and media put parenthood on a pedestal, enshrining it as the ideal goal for every girl and boy. We often think of it as the only proper role for any respectable citizen. That's not true. Fatherhood is the highest honor, but for many men, that honor comes from understanding that there are different aspects of fatherhood. Some of these can be fulfilled without having any children.

# AM I DAD OR UNCLE DAD?

A lot of things might go into a man's decision not to father children. Some men can't. They might try, but there are cases when a man's body doesn't produce the right mix of cells for reproduction. This doesn't mean these men can't be dads, but if that's what they want, they must do it by different means. Some men get involved with women who have children and become stepfathers. Increasing numbers of couples have success with medical options, such as in vitro fertilization. Then there are childless couples who adopt. If a man adopts a child, he takes on all the responsibilities we've been describing. An adoptive father is as real a dad as any biological father.

That's the commitment he makes, and the law enforces it. That's as real as it gets.

But some men don't want to be real dads. Why? There will always be a few men who simply don't like kids. They don't like kids' games, or kids' questions, or their immature personalities. These men aren't just indifferent to kids. They consciously avoid them. Some men are deeply afraid of young people. This condition has two names. First, there is pediophobia (not to be confused with the crime of pedophilia), which is a fear of infants and children. Its companion is ephebiphobia, or fear of teenagers. There are no accurate statistics about those who suffer from these afflictions, but studies indicate they are not as rare as we might imagine. Some researchers think both ailments affect our whole culture, but individual cases have been identified and diagnosed, and most of these are men. Though a man who doesn't like children at all seems to be missing something, as long as he doesn't harm them, there's little room for criticism. Of course, a man who suffers from either of these conditions should never become a father.

Most men who avoid fatherhood have nothing against children. They simply aren't interested in coming home to the responsibilities of a family. That doesn't mean they can't have a role in kids' lives. They share the same community with many children, so the potential is always there. Often, they even like kids, and interact well with them.

A lot of men who like kids simply aren't interested in becoming fathers. Some want to wait before starting a family, while others don't have any intention of ever becoming dads. Many people find this latter attitude odd, and even disturbing, especially in someone who seems to appreciate children. It shouldn't be. Quite a few men who avoid fatherhood still find good, constructive reasons to play positive, meaningful roles in kids' lives. First, it's a good and decent thing to do. Setting the right example for children isn't just a parenting skill; it's a mark of good citizenship. But what can a man do beyond that? Some childless men teach others to coach, and still, others act as surrogate dads in all kinds of circumstances. Some just form healthy friendships with the children in their lives.

These men aren't obligated to do anything. If a single, childless man doesn't take any interest in the young people of his community, he is well within his rights. But if such a man does take an interest, he must also accept some obligations. In all his interactions with children, he must act responsibly. The most important thing he must learn is how this responsibility works.

Often these kinds of contacts and relationships begin inside the family. If this man has younger siblings, cousins, or nieces and nephews, his duties begin with them. Most families expect older sons to take some responsibility for their younger siblings. The same often goes for cousins, and sometimes other kids in the neighborhood. Sometimes parents turn to an older son to babysit his younger brothers and sisters.

This young man might oversee getting his siblings to school or taking care of them at certain times of the day. An older brother or cousin is often expected to teach his younger relatives. He might coach his brothers in informal games. He could teach a younger sister how to read, or cook a meal, or use a smartphone.

As he gets older, these activities often extend beyond the family. In school, older boys are expected to be good role models for their younger schoolmates. Many teachers try to get older students to coach or tutor younger ones. A ninth-grader with a talent for math might be asked to help a fourth-grader who has a problem understanding division and multiplication. When the older boy does this, he needs to bring several fatherly qualities to the task. He must be patient and caring, but demanding, too. If the child gets the wrong answer, this older boy should not get upset, but he also can't ignore it. He must calmly help the child work through the problem until the child gets the right answer. By the time they are done, the older boy will have taught the child some math, but he also will have demonstrated how a mature teenager is supposed to act toward children. In fact, that demonstration may be the most important lesson the child receives in this transaction.

As the boy grows into manhood, he's bound to think a lot about becoming a father. Most mature single men think of the women in their lives as potential wives and mothers. But if a man decides fatherhood isn't in his immediate future, yet he still wants to spend quality time with kids, there are plenty of opportunities. If he has nieces and nephews, his opportunities begin with them. Are any of them growing up without dads? If so, he can play an essential role. It can start with the same things a responsible older brother does when he looks after them whenever their mothers can't.

The idea of a man taking over where there is no dad is as old as the family itself. Even Jesus had a stepdad: Mary's husband, Joseph. Joseph accepted this relationship, and helped guide Christ into adulthood, just as any father would do. Many famous people, from Booker T. Washington to Bill Clinton to John Lennon, had stepdads. President Barack Obama's biological father and mother divorced when he was still a small child. Not long after that, his mother married again. Her husband, Lolo Soetoro, was the future president's stepfather from the time Obama was four until he reached his teens. Once, when young Barack had trouble with bullies at school, Soetoro taught him to box. At the same time, this man cautioned the young boy to be fair and just. His manner was gentle, but his direction was firm. He wanted the boy to find his inner strength. Obama later said of him: "...my stepfather was a good man who gave me some things that were very helpful."

In an earlier chapter, we mentioned the fathering skills of President John F. Kennedy's dad. Old Joe Kennedy had taught his sons well, a fact that grew in importance when tragedy struck the family. As we all know, his oldest living son, the president, was assassinated when he was only forty-six. Joe Kennedy had always taught his children that if one of them died, another must take over that one's role in the family. This applied to both public and private lives.

We all know how this worked publicly. JFK didn't go into politics until his older brother, Joe, Jr., was killed in World War II. When JFK died, his young brother, Robert, pursued the late president's policy goals. When Robert was cut down, their youngest brother, Ted, took up their cause. But as that was happening, a similar process was playing out in the privacy of their family. When JFK died, he left two small children: Caroline, six, and John, Jr., who was not yet three. Robert took over as their father figure. With eight children of his own (eventually, he would father eleven), Robert was no stranger to the responsibilities of fatherhood. Less than five years later, after Robert's death, the duties of surrogate fatherhood passed to

Ted. When he took over Robert's role, he acted as a father to an entire generation of Kennedy kids. Two became congressmen, while others worked as lawyers, publishers, entrepreneurs, and authors. Now, as their children become adults, the Kennedys are still one of the most famous families in the world.

When a man is deciding whether he wants to start a family, he must ask himself: What kind of man am I? Am I a man who likes living with other people? Do I like children? Do I feel a commitment to them? A man must choose his commitments carefully. He might like kids and enjoy living in the same house with them, but fatherhood is far more than having a new set of housemates. When a man decides to become a father, he's doing it for a lifetime. This bond isn't broken by divorce or even the death of the child's mom. Those kinds of tragedies often make a father-child connection grow stronger.

The man who wants to help parents with their kids, but doesn't want to be a dad, must accept some of a dad's responsibilities. He must be honest with these children, yet he must shield them from some things they haven't yet learned. He must protect them from harm yet correct them if they are about to harm others.

For the majority of men, the decision not to have kids doesn't have to be final. Most men start their adult lives, saying: "Not yet." Many of us keep saying that right up to the moment of truth when a girlfriend, fiancée, or wife says: "I'm pregnant with our baby." Only then do we finally face up to our obligations.

Being "Uncle Dad" is often the best preparation for fatherhood, especially if the commitment is real but limited. It might work something like this: You don't want to start a family yet, but your best friend already has. He and his wife have a six-year-old boy and a four-year-old girl. Your friend's National Guard unit gets called up, and he has to spend a year in a war zone. The night before he deploys, he asks you to keep an eye on his kids and help them while he's absent.

If his wife agrees, and you accept, you are taking on many of the responsibilities of being a father. Your friend's son will be going through a pivotal year, starting first grade, as he takes those initial steps beyond the boundaries of home and neighborhood. He will make new friends at school, and not all of them will be good influences. You will want to talk to this young boy and listen to everything he says. If he's learning negative lessons, you should correct them. If he's having problems in his classes, you must be sensitive, but also firm.

The same thing goes for the friend's young daughter. You must help her understand and respect the obligations that have taken her father away from her. You should assure her that he will return as soon as he's able. And you must communicate all this in a way that a four-year-old can accept.

You must also help their mother, but avoid crossing any boundaries. If she's attractive, you should train yourself to resist temptation. But you should also make sure she knows you are there to help with those kids. Their health and happiness should be your only concern.

This is the kind of situation where a responsible young man can make a big difference even though he's not yet a dad. He's committed himself to help raise another man's children for a limited amount of time. He's taken on certain duties, but they won't last forever. He might have a girlfriend or even a fiancée. He may feel some pressure from the woman in his life, or from others, to settle down, marry, and have kids. Yet he's not sure. Here's his chance to find out what kind of father he would be.

This isn't really fatherhood. A man in this position must answer to the kids' dad, and he must also heed the mother's wishes. Either of them can end his role in their children's lives in an instant. Whatever authority he has comes from them. They grant him access, and they constantly monitor his actions. No matter how much trust they give him, these are their kids, and the kids will always come first.

Yet he does have some authority to go with his obligations. If he's the only adult in the house, the kids must listen to him and obey any instruction that won't bring them to harm. Even when their mom, or other adults, are present, this substitute dad plays a special role with these children. Their real father has given him a huge trust, and their mother has agreed to it. She knows that if she contradicts what he says, in her kids' eyes, it will weaken him. She won't do that unless she feels it's absolutely necessary. She wants a good man in her children's lives.

This is one example of an "Uncle Dad" situation. There are plenty of others, and everyone is different. Some "Uncle Dads" are real uncles. Some are boyfriends of single moms who haven't yet entered the family circle. Often ministers and teachers fill the role of "Uncle Dad." Or it might just be a trusted neighbor.

If you find that a child's parents have accepted you as being an "Uncle Dad" to their kids, you have already jumped over one big hurdle. These people are willing to trust you with their most important responsibilities. For most parents, that's a very big thing. Think about it. If you had children, who would you trust enough to supervise them?

"Uncle Dad" is a good role for any man who's considering the question of whether he wants to be a father. A man who takes on this obligation is something like a late-season call-up on a major league baseball team that's still in contention for a playoff spot. The ballplayer is trying out, but he's doing it in real games that count. So is "Uncle Dad." If the player makes some mistakes, he has teammates who will come to his rescue. If he does just about everything wrong, the team sends him back to the minors. "Uncle Dad" has one or both parents who will soon be there to back him up or take care of any problems he can't handle.

But for some men, "Uncle Dad" becomes a permanent role. It might be like this with one family, or it might be a man's relationship with several families, along with quite a few kids. Men who take on this role with multiple families are often just doing their jobs. These are the teachers and ministers we've mentioned, as well as coaches, counselors, and others who work with children.

If you want to try the role of "Uncle Dad," but no one has offered it to you, there are several routes you might take. One is to let friends and relatives know you're available to help with their kids. If you do this, and none of them accept the offer, ask them why, and assure them you want an honest answer. They might see evidence of immaturity in some of your words and actions—immaturity you weren't even aware of. Or it might just be that they already have it covered.

If the former is true, listen to what they say, and do some soul-searching. A part of maturity is accepting criticism and acting to correct the problem. If you change your behavior, they might be more ready to let you help them with their kids.

If they already have an "Uncle Dad" available, then look for other opportunities. Check out your church, community center, or youth sports organizations. Are there any "Big Brother" programs in your area? If a man really wants to contribute his services, these organizations are always looking for volunteers.

Being an "Uncle Dad" has its limitations, but it's an important role that holds the potential for doing good for young people. It happens for many different reasons and takes many different forms. If you're ready, it's a great education about the experience of fatherhood.

# RESPONSIBILITY HAS NO SHELF LIFE

T he problem of absentee fathers will always be with us. Death, divorce, and abandonment won't ever go away. Some men will always leave, voluntarily or involuntarily, but the problem can be eased. We just need to work on it one dad, one mom, and one family at a time.

The responsibility for solving it is mainly on the shoulders of men, but women have a role in this, too. Women must give willing fathers and father figures the chance to connect with their children. Some women resist this, and it's easy to understand why. Most single mothers have seen their men leave. Most of these men made a conscious decision to go, giving up their families. They looked at their kids, found themselves face-to-face with a lifetime of obligations, and they fled. They left the mothers of their children with nothing. They abandoned their kids, dodged their support payments, and refused to accept any consequences. Who could blame a single mom for feeling bitter? If any man—her children's father, or some other potential dad—shows up at the door, who can blame her if she slams it in his face?

But there are times when she shouldn't.

Many single moms feel that men have no place in their lives. They're wrong. As we've pointed out, again and again, children who have a father in the house do better than children who don't. The numbers prove it. They get better grades, have fewer behavioral problems, and enjoy better health. As they get older, they're more likely to stay in school, avoid crime and drugs, and eventually, they get better jobs. These positive effects often remain through generations, as kids become parents and create new and stable families of their own.

That doesn't mean that a single mom should run out and grab the first man she finds. She probably did that before and remembered where it got her! This time she should be careful. When a man expresses interest in her, she should make sure he's interested in her kids, too. To pass this test, he must show that his interest is real, and can be sustained with even the slightest encouragement. She should give him a chance to show how he feels by bringing her kids into the conversation at the earliest opportunity. If she mentions that she'll have to be home for them by a certain hour, what's his reaction? Does he seem pleased at her concern for them? Or is he annoyed by it? When he first meets her kids, are they his focus? Or is he checking out their mom's reactions to his every move? Does he like these children? Do they like him? If so, is his affection real? Or does it seem more like an effort meant to impress her?

The test should continue over time. Mom should observe this man and her kids in as many situations as possible. Does he ignore them? Is he trying far too hard to be their pal? Does he try to buy their approval? How is he with Mom's authority over her kids? Does he try to take over? Or is he respectful, and supportive of her efforts? Can he sense when they really do need correction, and give it gently, but firmly? Does he fit into her family's dynamic? Or is he trying too hard?

Though no man will be perfect, when a single mom starts looking for a potential mate, she has every reason to be cautious. She's been burned before, and she should learn from that experience. She must be clear about what she wants from a man—clear about her own thoughts, and clear when she expresses them to him. In the past, she might've been swept away by tall, dark, and handsome. Now she needs to adjust those standards. She should be more concerned with his character than his looks. Rather than thinking about romantic trysts, she should wonder how he will look changing a diaper. Will he be irritated and resentful? Or is she amused at his own clumsiness in hitching up the Huggies?

The earlier chapters are full of clues about the qualities a woman should look for in a potential father. One of her first requirements is stability, both emotional and financial. A potential father should be able to remain calm, especially in a crisis. He should be steady, and able to deal with life's everyday dramas. He should have a good job that produces a reasonable paycheck. He doesn't have to be rich (though there's no reason why he can't be). He doesn't even have to make enough to support the whole family himself. That was the idea of another era. If he's willing and able to do his part and keep up his end of the financial bargain, this should not be a problem. With a dad in the picture, Mom can still work and contribute her share. But a potential father should help the family's financial situation, and not be a drain on its resources.

A good dad will help around the house. That doesn't mean he has to be a perfect housekeeper, but he should make a substantial effort. Maybe his specialty is repairing things or doing the big chores, like cleaning out the garage or basement. If there's a lawn, he should mow it; if there's a hedge, he should clip it. Or maybe he'll paint that bathroom, where the walls have been blistered and peeling for a couple of years now. Not all these tasks will come naturally to him, but he should be willing to do whatever he can. That's what good dads do.

He should also be ready to do whatever it takes to earn the children's respect and affection. If he's going to be a real dad to them, he must realize these are honors to be won, and not rights to be claimed. Like their mother, these kids have already fallen victim to a man who abandoned them. Whether this is that same man, saying that he's reformed, or a new man taking his place, he must always act in ways that earn their trust. He can make a big effort, taking them places, bringing them gifts, and helping them with their problems, but if he doesn't tell them the truth, and demonstrate that he's there for them for the long haul, he's not the man Mom's looking for.

A good dad knows the value of quality time. He understands that children need a dad who will listen. He should enjoy spending time with kids. He should pay attention to what they do and say and be interested in their ideas. As he finds his place in the family, he should help them with homework, and encourage them in their after-school activities.

As Mom and her kids gain confidence in this man, he must gently assert himself in his gradually emerging role of father and husband. He might begin by talking with Mom about the family finances and ask what he can contribute. Some women are too proud and/or suspicious to let a man pay for anything. At times this is wise, but if Mom is letting this guy stick around, and if that's costing her money, she should see what happens if she lets him start paying his own way.

Is he serious? If and when he does pay, does he start expecting special treatment? If the money never materializes, or if he thinks it buys him the right to take over the house, then it's time for him to hit the road. But if he goes slowly, and lives up to his obligations without getting heavy-handed, Mom might see this man as a keeper!

Once he starts paying his share of the bills, Mom should listen to whatever he has to say about money and property. She doesn't have to agree with him on everything, nor does she have to hand over any control—yet. This process should be gradual, and she should set her own pace. But if this potential dad is paying his fair share, and if he proves himself to be stable, thrifty, and sensible, Mom should recognize that he might be a good partner for the future.

A good man won't walk in and try to exert his authority over the children. In the beginning, he doesn't have any, and when Mom cedes some of her authority to him, he must exercise it with careful respect for her wishes. A new man in the family needs to recognize that the most effective way to channel kids' behavior in the right direction is to lead by example. If he does the right thing, they are far more likely to do the right thing, too. Sometimes this takes a conscious effort, but it should usually be automatic. If he's the kind of person who always has to wonder about what's right and what's wrong, that should be a warning. Fairness and decency should be habits. If they are, this man will automatically show your children how to make the right choices.

Any candidate for fatherhood should be brave enough to demonstrate his love in many ways, big and small. He shouldn't be afraid of making his emotions known. Emotional honesty is one way to describe this. This doesn't mean a man has to turn to mush, nor does he have to behave in what many would call a "touchy-feely" manner. He just must be willing to let the people around him know his real emotional response to situations and events. Men who make a habit of hiding their emotions often allow hostility and anger to build up inside them. These negative feelings need an outlet, or they will eat a man up from within, sometimes resulting in violence, or psychological breakdown.

A good dad must be committed enough to Mom and the kids that he's willing to plan for and invest in the future of his family. This is important in a financial sense, but it's not just about money. Much of his investment is in the form of mature emotional commitment. He should discuss the family's future needs with Mom, and together, they should make the key decisions. These include choices about where the family will live, what schools the children will attend, and employment possibilities for both parents.

In most cases, these kinds of conversations won't take place right at the beginning of a relationship. They should develop gradually, as talk about hopes and dreams develops into a detailed discussion of concrete, here-and-now issues. When it reaches the point where the man is included in decisions about household spending, then both should feel more comfortable about sharing their thoughts about the future. Investment in the future is a commitment that's required of any real father.

When a man gets involved with a woman, his initial attraction is often somewhat shallow and self-serving. His thoughts are usually about their date, and where it might lead on that very night. That's natural, and no man should be blamed for it. But as time passes, if they get involved with each other, this should change. If the budding relationship is a healthy one, both people will have evolving thoughts about each other.

Mom will look at just about any man she goes out with as something more than just a casual companion for an evening. Right away, she will look for signs showing whether he's a potential mate and father. A man might realize he's getting this scrutiny. If so, what's his reaction? Most men automatically seek pleasure. Can this one set his physical urges aside, long enough to see who Mom really is? Does he understand the importance of her family? There's nothing wrong with a man having selfish urges, but when Mom looks past those, she should be able to see some sign that he's interested in her, and the life she's living. When he meets her kids, he should show some understanding of their wants and needs.

As time passes, this should develop into a sense of selflessness. As a man gets serious, he needs to make sacrifices for his family. Is this man willing to do that?

Some men seem willing to support a family, help with the kids, and make decisions. These men often appear to make a full commitment to what Mom wants. But as soon as Mom starts letting this man exert any authority at all, he tries to take over. Of course, he'll support the family. He'll move them into a better house, pay for better schooling, and make sure their every need is met. But he also has set ideas about what he's paying for. This is the man who believes that a father always knows best, and no one attempts to contradict him. To him, Mom is only another child looking for direction. He believes that once he's supporting them, they are beholden to him. This man might have a desperate need for a family, but a good family has no need of him.

Even if Mom finds a wealthy man who can pay for all those things, she shouldn't give up her place in her family's decision-making. Her life and kids are her own. She has her own beliefs and values, and they shouldn't be for sale. Money can't buy moral authority. A man can only get that by earning it with honesty, compassion, and fairness.

Often a mom can tell a lot about a man's moral character by looking at his faith. Of course, many people prefer mates whose religious beliefs are compatible with theirs, but any man's commitment to the Almighty should help make him a better man. He should understand that the world is ruled by a greater power. In this spirit, he should recognize that fatherhood is about more than just himself, Mom, and the children. What they are creating is a foundation for generations yet unborn. While there are no guarantees, families that live honest, decent lives have a better chance of passing those qualities on. This is how our core values survive and thrive.

All parents are responsible for the next generation. That's why it's so important to get involved in churches, schools, and other community activities that bring parents and children together to do God's work. Families create communities in those places.

Some good men aren't cut out for a life of home and kids. A good man might go out on that date with Mom, show genuine interest in the kids, but then realize that this family stuff is not for him. He might not be ready yet, or maybe he'll never be ready. If he realizes this and is honest about it, Mom shouldn't totally reject him. She should do all she can to welcome him as a friend. She can encourage any positive relationships he might form with her children. Until she finds the right man—and even after—this man can serve as "Uncle Dad."

In far too many communities, the problem of absentee fathers is a scourge. Some of these dads will never be reformed. If they aren't willing to face their responsibilities, they should bow out of their families' lives, leaving the way clear for men who are willing to stay and fulfill their commitments. Those who can get past their selfish whims, and learn to take on these responsibilities, should do so carefully, and always with respect for Mom and the children.

Other young, single men should do all they can to become the kinds of fathers that families desperately need. Some will find single, childless women, and start new families with them. Others will find themselves interested in women, only to find that children are already a part of the package. This shouldn't scare them off. A good mom is a treasure, and raising kids is the most rewarding job of all.

All men face the decision of whether to become a father. We should see it as our greatest opportunity and honor, one we need to be prepared for. Those of us who don't become fathers need to help our friends who are dads, giving them support in every way possible. Those of us who are dads must honor our wives and children by giving them the best we have to offer. It's the one investment that's guaranteed to enrich all of us for the rest of our lives.

# About the Author

Malcolm Allen is a recognized expert on human potential and (BCSA) Board Certified Social Advocate. He migrates effortlessly between corporate boardrooms and underserved communities aiming to advance the interests of social justice, particularly on behalf of populations or groups who have been disadvantaged, disempowered, or forgotten.

Allen has authored over two dozen books, and most have achieved best-selling status. He has worked with subject matter experts and credentialed instruction designers to socially engineer a platform of outcome-based programs that provide solutions for disabled veterans, recidivism, human trafficking, dropout prevention, bullying, diversity, mentoring, financial inclusion, entrepreneurship, and leadership. All programs are Military Approved, and available at Penn Foster College and Graduate America Centers of Excellence around the world. For seminar licensing, book purchases, or speaker requests, please visit: Unconditional.org